"I'M ACTUALLY MUCH SCARIER IN PERSON"

another collection of comics, paintings and junk

I0135937

by damian willcox

introduction

tom brickner, fifth grade. if you were to ask me the circumstances of my introduction to drawing, this is what i would tell you. i clearly remember it even **MANY** years later: the moment my classmate showed me all of the drawings in the back of his school notebook. there was no art class in sight, no tubs of paint, or smocks or class assignments. he didn't **HAVE** to draw - he was drawing - on his own...because he wanted to! i was intrigued, and began making small doodles of sneakers, and the classic medieval sword in the stone, as well as other such mismatched topics that have no right being together in the back of my own notebook - as tom had assured me we would never reach the back of the book with class notes, so it was a safe location to draw in. in the years that followed i continued to draw, at times it thrived and other times sputtered along.

when college came along (no, not art school) one of my courses involved piping drafting...i loved it. the craft and lost art of manual drafting with pencil and paper, but the best part of the class was the instructor. every day he would walk into the room, give some instruction, answer some questions, help where needed, and then inevitably...unquestionably...and without fail, walk up to the chalkboard and etch these three awe inspiring words that have become so deeply ingrained in me: "draw like mad". i guess i took these words to heart - not just then, but ever since then. i mean...i had drawn before that, but it was around this time that i created my very first dorkboy comic, as well as introduced myself to acrylic painting by way of affordable paints from across the campus at the neighbouring art school's bookstore...and it has definitely not slowed down since.

the book you hold in your hands represents countless hours spent , numerous late nights, far too many cups of tea, very few hours of sleep and most of all, it represents me... drawing...drawing like mad.

♥damian

"The Hunter"

damian

"the hunter"
(clip studio paint pro)
i'm pretty sure this is how nature views humans.

"the return of fat ninja!"
(clip studio paint pro)

"mental self portrait"
(clip studio paint pro)

"cream of the crop circles"
(adobe ideas on ipad)

"Dr. Wilson couldn't be sure where his calculations had gone wrong"

"dr. wilson couldn't be sure where his calculations had gone wrong"
(sketchtime on ipad)

i drew this with my finger in a matter of minutes, and it taught me once again that time spent vs reader enjoyment is subjective and can be inversely proportional as it garnered the most visits to my website EVER.

"the vegetarian fish"
(and the confident worm)
(clip studio paint pro)
i have a strong suspicion that not all fish like worms.
of course, based on my past fishing experiences they
don't seem fond of corn either.

WHERE SOYMILK COMES FROM

damian 2012

"soymilk origins"
(ink & watercolour on small paper)
just be glad i didn't draw a whole pasture of
soybeans hooked up to milking machines...shudder.

"rolling with the plunges"
(ink & watercolour on small paper)
try not to think about how awkward this would be in real life.

dr. bill's monster...

The story of "dr. bill" is a sordid one - most notably due to the fact that he is in fact a "bill", but most undeniably not a doctor.

This particular short comic story arc partially began based on a set of pseudonyms given to real life former coworkers, and much like other comics I have done sort of took on a life all of its own.

I expect you will see more of these characters in the future (and more), but in the meantime if your doctor's name is "Bill"... I would suggest a second opinion.

(ink & watercolour for all)

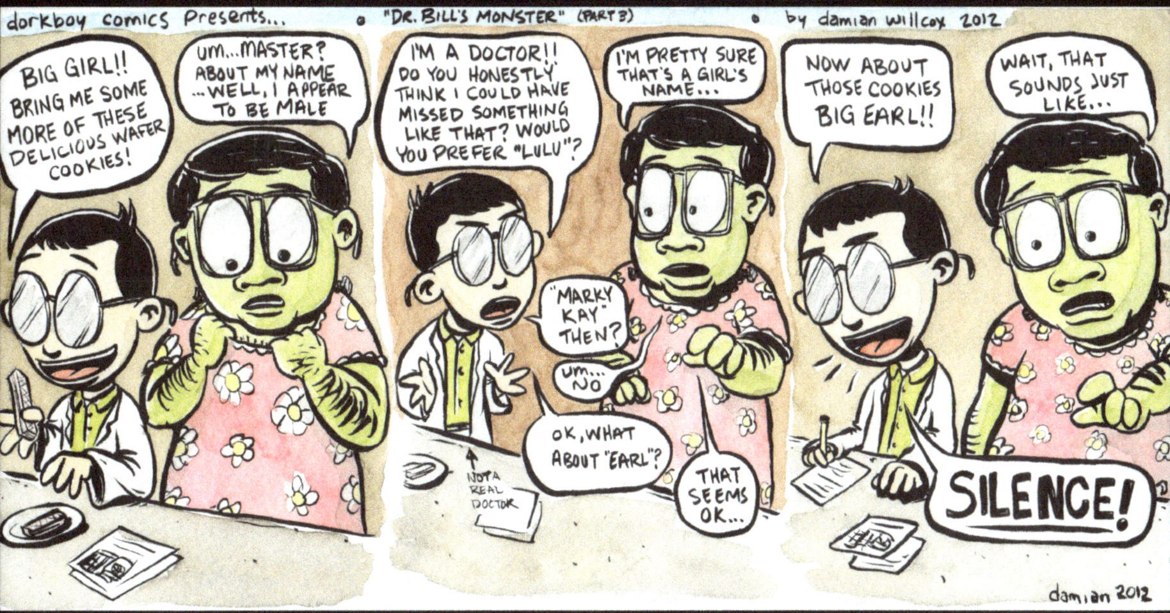
dorkboy comics presents... • "DR. BILL'S MONSTER" (PART 3) • by damian willcox 2012
BIG GIRL!! BRING ME SOME MORE OF THESE DELICIOUS WAFER COOKIES!
UM...MASTER? ABOUT MY NAME ...WELL, I APPEAR TO BE MALE
I'M A DOCTOR!! DO YOU HONESTLY THINK I COULD HAVE MISSED SOMETHING LIKE THAT? WOULD YOU PREFER "LULU"?
I'M PRETTY SURE THAT'S A GIRL'S NAME...
"MARKY KAY" THEN?
UM... NO
OK, WHAT ABOUT "EARL"?
NOT A REAL DOCTOR
THAT SEEMS OK...
NOW ABOUT THOSE COOKIES BIG EARL!!
WAIT, THAT SOUNDS JUST LIKE...
SILENCE!
damian 2012
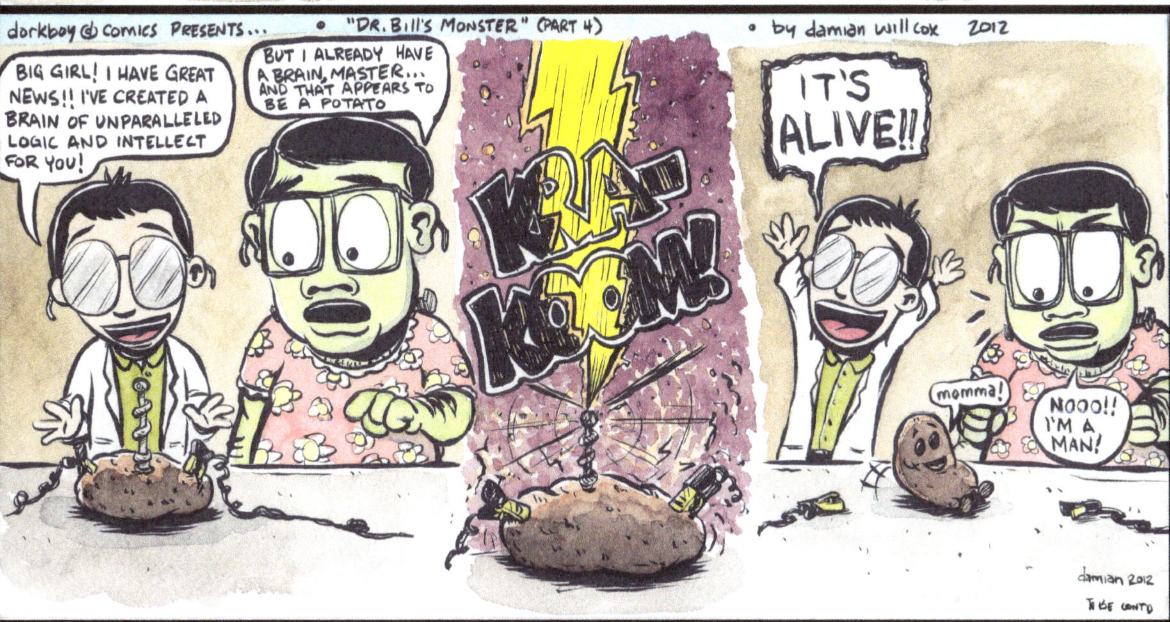
dorkboy comics PRESENTS... • "DR. Bill's MONSTER" (PART 4) • by damian willcox 2012
BIG GIRL! I HAVE GREAT NEWS!! I'VE CREATED A BRAIN OF UNPARALLELED LOGIC AND INTELLECT FOR YOU!
BUT I ALREADY HAVE A BRAIN, MASTER... AND THAT APPEARS TO BE A POTATO
KRA-KOOM!
IT'S ALIVE!!
momma!
NOOO!! I'M A MAN!
damian 2012
TO BE CONTD
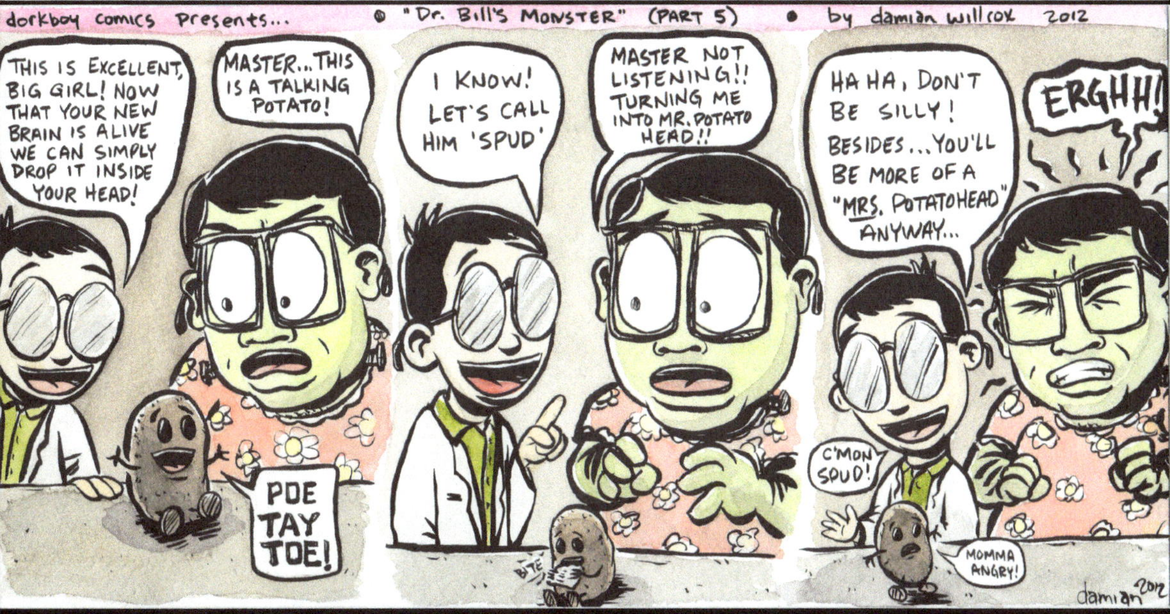
dorkboy comics presents... • "Dr. Bill's MONSTER" (PART 5) • by damian willcox 2012
THIS IS EXCELLENT, BIG GIRL! NOW THAT YOUR NEW BRAIN IS ALIVE WE CAN SIMPLY DROP IT INSIDE YOUR HEAD!
MASTER...THIS IS A TALKING POTATO!
POE TAY TOE!
I KNOW! LET'S CALL HIM 'SPUD'
MASTER NOT LISTENING!! TURNING ME INTO MR. POTATO HEAD!!
BITE
HA HA, DON'T BE SILLY! BESIDES...YOU'LL BE MORE OF A "MRS. POTATOHEAD" ANYWAY...
ERGHH!
C'MON SPUD!
MOMMA ANGRY!
damian 2012

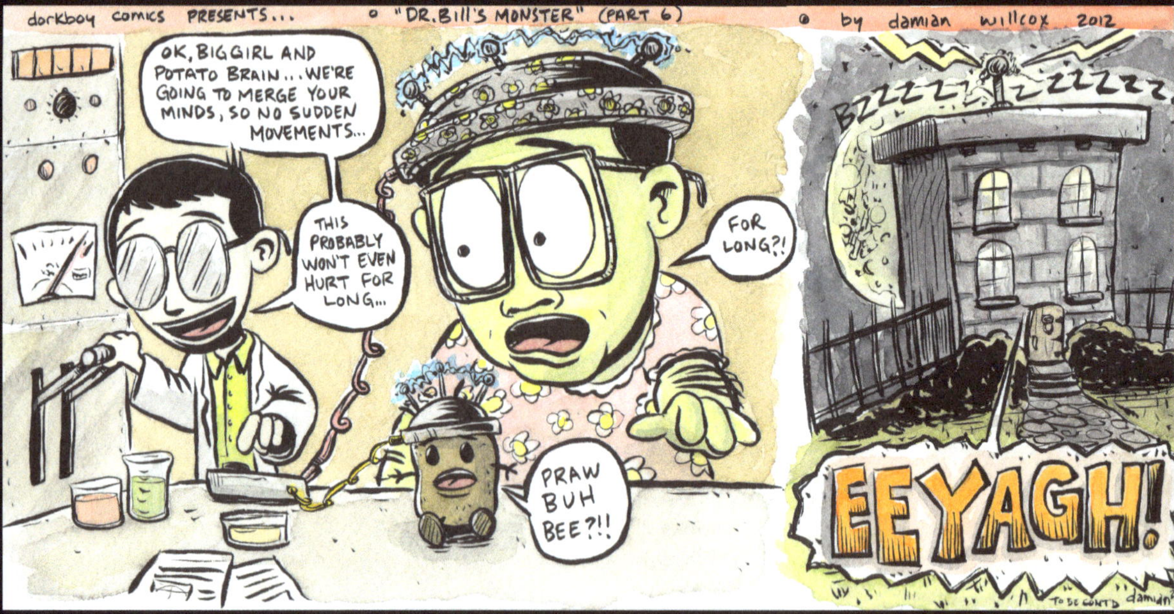

dorkboy comics PRESENTS... "DR. BILL'S MONSTER" (PART 6) by damian willcox 2012
OK, BIGGIRL AND POTATO BRAIN... WE'RE GOING TO MERGE YOUR MINDS, SO NO SUDDEN MOVEMENTS...
THIS PROBABLY WON'T EVEN HURT FOR LONG...
FOR LONG?!
PRAW BUH BEE?!!
BZZZZZZZZZZZ
EEYAGH!
TO BE CONT'D damian

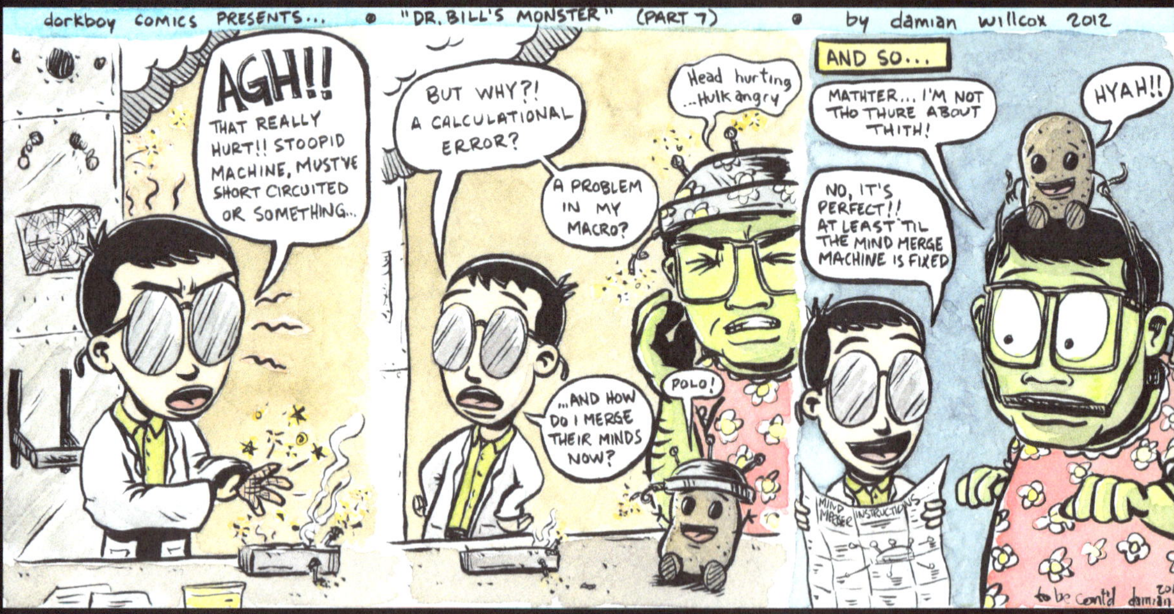

dorkboy comics PRESENTS... "DR. BILL'S MONSTER" (PART 7) by damian willcox 2012
AGH!! THAT REALLY HURT!! STOOPID MACHINE, MUST'VE SHORT CIRCUITED OR SOMETHING...
BUT WHY?! A CALCULATIONAL ERROR?
A PROBLEM IN MY MACRO?
Head hurting ...Hulk angry
...AND HOW DO I MERGE THEIR MINDS NOW?
POLO!
AND SO...
MATHTER... I'M NOT THO THURE ABOUT THITH!
HYAH!!
NO, IT'S PERFECT!! AT LEAST 'TIL THE MIND MERGE MACHINE IS FIXED
MIND MERGER INSTRUCTIONS
to be cont'd damian

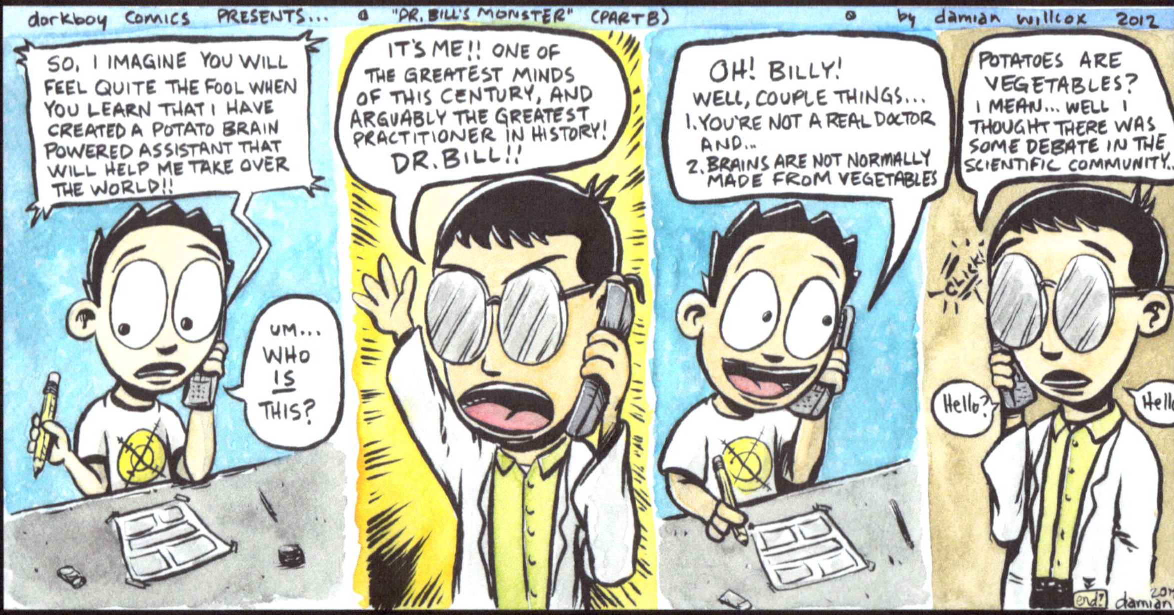

dorkboy comics PRESENTS... "DR. BILL'S MONSTER" (PART 8) by damian willcox 2012
SO, I IMAGINE YOU WILL FEEL QUITE THE FOOL WHEN YOU LEARN THAT I HAVE CREATED A POTATO BRAIN POWERED ASSISTANT THAT WILL HELP ME TAKE OVER THE WORLD!!
UM... WHO IS THIS?
IT'S ME!! ONE OF THE GREATEST MINDS OF THIS CENTURY, AND ARGUABLY THE GREATEST PRACTITIONER IN HISTORY! DR. BILL!!
OH! BILLY! WELL, COUPLE THINGS... 1. YOU'RE NOT A REAL DOCTOR AND.. 2. BRAINS ARE NOT NORMALLY MADE FROM VEGETABLES
POTATOES ARE VEGETABLES? I MEAN... WELL I THOUGHT THERE WAS SOME DEBATE IN THE SCIENTIFIC COMMUNITY...
CLICK!
Hello?
Hello
end! damian

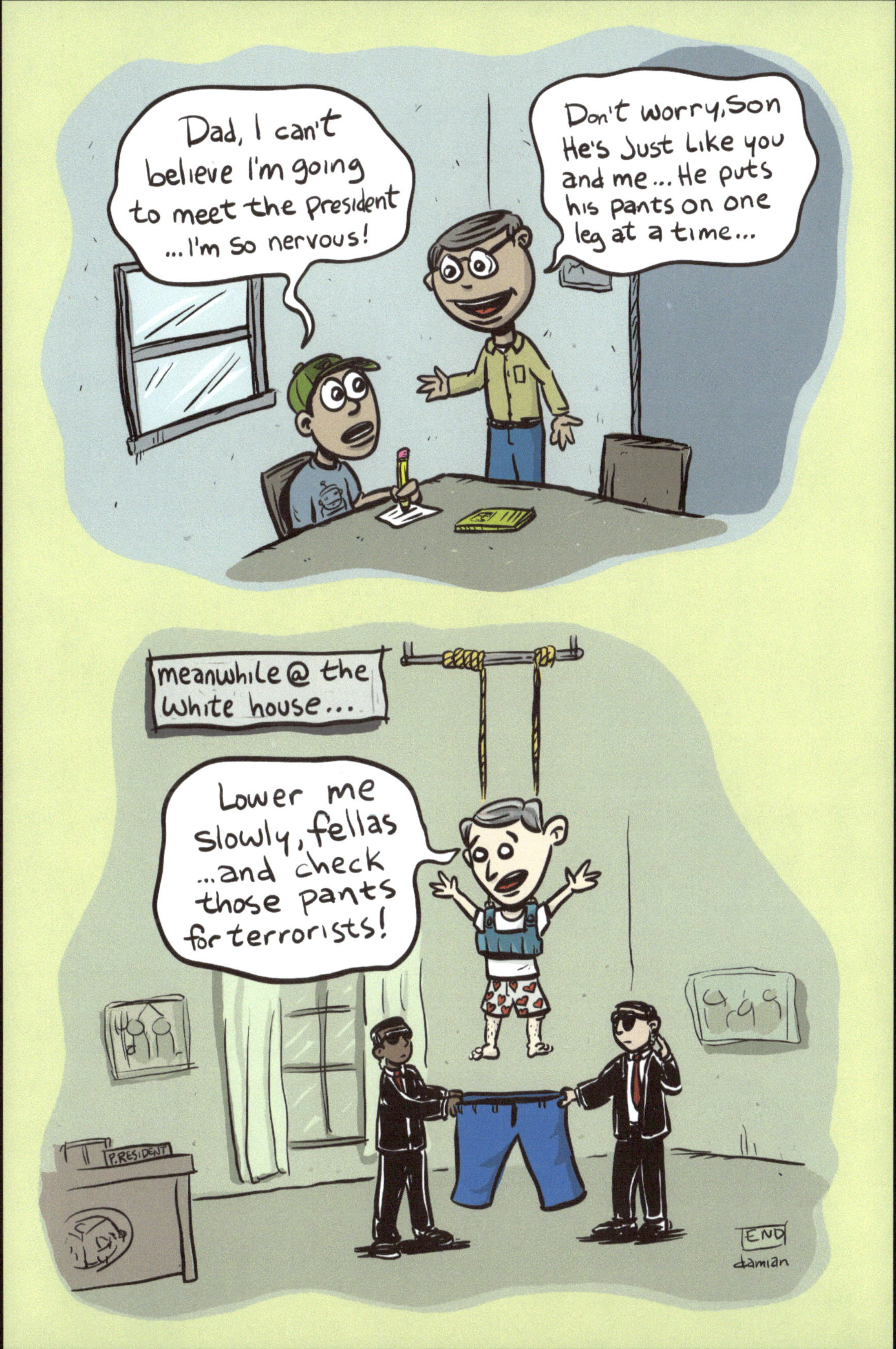
Dad, I can't believe I'm going to meet the President ...I'm So nervous!
Don't worry, Son He's Just like you and me... He puts his pants on one leg at a time...
meanwhile @ the White house...
Lower me slowly, fellas ...and check those pants for terrorists!
P.RESIDENT
END
damian

(adobe illustrator)
you really need to imagine the accent to do this justice...

and then one day, without warning, everyone's batteries died...

...and the earth stood still.

...briefly.

Zombies attacked the wrong city...

Godzilla was distracted...

Nope, wrong again! this time keep your eye on the marble...

↘ shell game

the Aliens were caught in traffic...

BEEP!

HONK!

I BRAKE 4 HUMANS

...Once again, earth was safe.

damian [end]

"the gravity of the situation"
(ink & watercolour)

space...

"Neil"

"a better moon landing"

"final frontier"
(ink & watercolour)

"life is short…"

a matter of perspective"
(ink & watercolour)

TWO DAYS AGO, I GAVE MY WIFE FLOWERS FOR OUR NINTH WEDDING ANNIVERSARY

TODAY, MY WIFE GAVE ME FLOWERS FOR THE DEATH OF MY GRANDMOTHER

MAYBE ALL OF THOSE FLOWER PAINTINGS I COMPLAIN ABOUT AREN'T SO STUPID AFTER ALL...

"flower power"
(ink & watercolour)

SORRY SIR, WE ONLY ALLOW ONE CARRION PER PASSENGER

© WWW.DORKBOYCOMICS.COM

damian

i still miss him mom

SPOT

oh sweetie, he's never really gone if you keep him in your heart

Later...

c'mere boy!

end

i guess i have no more grand parents. bye grandma...

19

"intelligent insects"

perhaps it's time we stopped looking on <u>other</u> planets for intelligent life?

(adobe illustrator)

despite the last few pages seeming a bit morbid, one of the things i love about comics is their ability to bring sensitive topics to the table. when i originally made the comic to the left several years back, i heard back from a reader that they were going to pass it along to a family member that was having a particularly difficult time with the disease. it's hearing things like this that truly keep me going.

"daily dose"
(sketchtime on ipad)

"how's this for a snappy title?"
bridgeland, calgary
(ink, watercolour, and careless brush splatter)

BRIDGELAND
CHURCH
July 7 2012
22

damian

sketchcrawlin'

sketchcrawls entail heading out with little more than a sketchbook and a few art supplies, and drawing things on location.

This section collects some of the places i have done this in my hometown of Calgary, as well as a little later in this book where i have some work from Japan.

check out www.sketchcrawl.com to find one in your area!

"the pulpit & the powerlines"
bridgeland, calgary
(ink & watercolour)

"school's out"
calgary, ab
(ink & watercolour)
24

"calgary peace bridge"
(ink & watercolour)

"miyuki & lychee"
bowness park, calgary

"bowness park"
calgary, ab

foliage...

as long as i can remember, i have drawn trees in my sketchbooks . one time while drawing on the bus, a lady saw me sketching a tree and told me that it means "i'm growing".

"dr. seuss tree"
devonian gardens, calgary, ab
(ink & watercolour)

page: "view from city hall"

...and 'zillas

as long as i can remember, i have drawn 'zillas and inserted them randomly into comic stories.

"dogzilla", "popezilla", you name it, they have ended up in comics or sketches, and continue to do so.

in this particular sketching outing, i decided this location needed a garden variety 'zilla added to spice up the locale.

...i wonder what that lady would have said about this.

"hey, what's for lunch?"
devonian gardens,
calgary, ab
(ink & watercolour)

"godzilla vs medical school"
(ink & watercolour)

'zillas attack!

"godzilla's most memorable battle yet"
(ink & watercolour on small paper)
i still question if not including high waisted pants on this one
was a mistake...these are the things that keep me up at night.

"frosty the snowzilla"
(ink & watercolour on small paper)
i know, i know...you have questions.
no, i don't think he can breathe fire...he'll melt.

"atlantiszilla"
(ink & watercolour on small paper)

i created "atlantiszilla" at approximately midnight by the light of a desk lamp in a hotel room in the city of miyazaki, japan.

i remember the night very clearly, as shortly before this i braved the somewhat rainy evening to visit an enormous 24 hour bookstore just blocks away, and spent what seemed like nowhere near enough time poring over the vast selection of painting and illustration books, unseen in north america. afterwards, i returned to the hotel and drew this.

"penguinzilla"
(ink & watercolour)

MIDNIGHT SNACK

"midnight snack"
(bamboopaper on ipad)

SURPRISE INSIDE!

"surprise inside
(adobe illustrato

"future career options"
(adobe illustrator)

Count Broccula...

"count broccula"
(ink & watercolour)

...and other scary stories.

this section attempts to collect the various monstrosities i have brought into this world through the use of pen, paper and tesla coils...er...i mean...forget i said anything....

"frankly, mrs. shankly"
(watercolour pencil crayons)

the Ghost of Laundry Day

2012
damian

"the ghost of laundry day"
(ink & watercolour)
there's something incredible about being able to transform
anyone or anything into a supernatural monster of sorts
simply by throwing a bedsheet over it. had there been
more time, i assure you there would have been more ghost
drawings....many more.

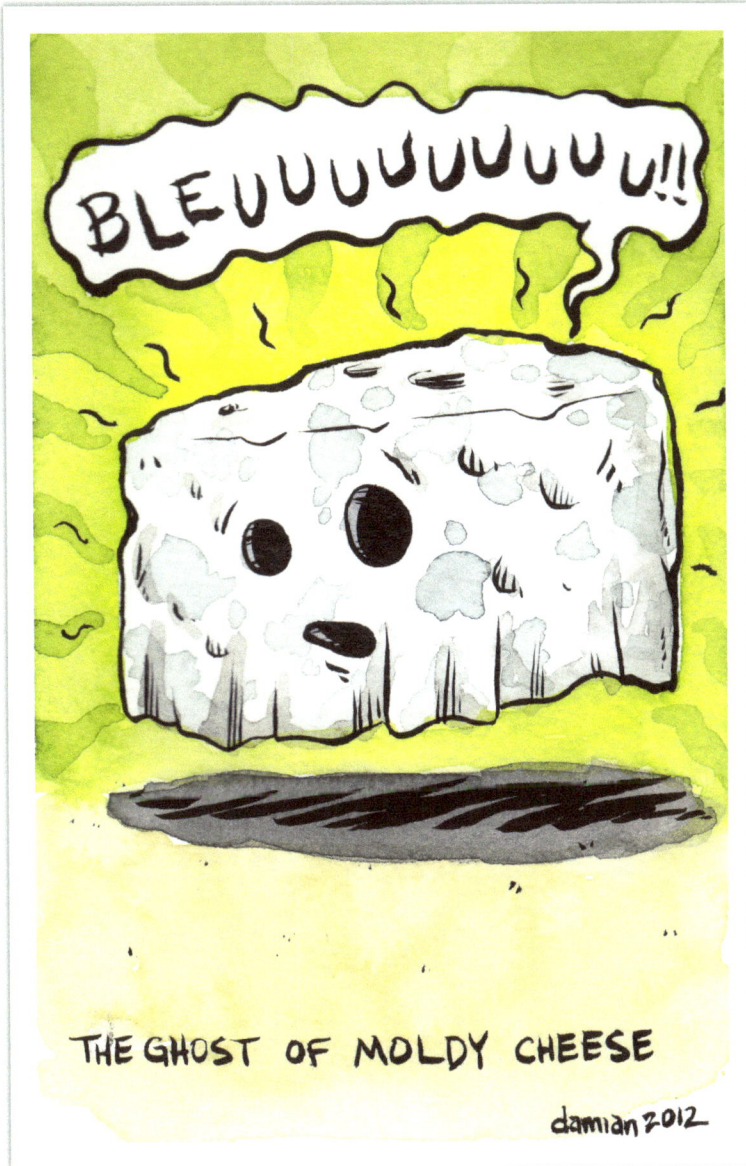

"have a gouda halloween"
(ink & watercolour)
this in dedication to the unholiest of cheeses...bleu cheese.
don't believe me? google some images.

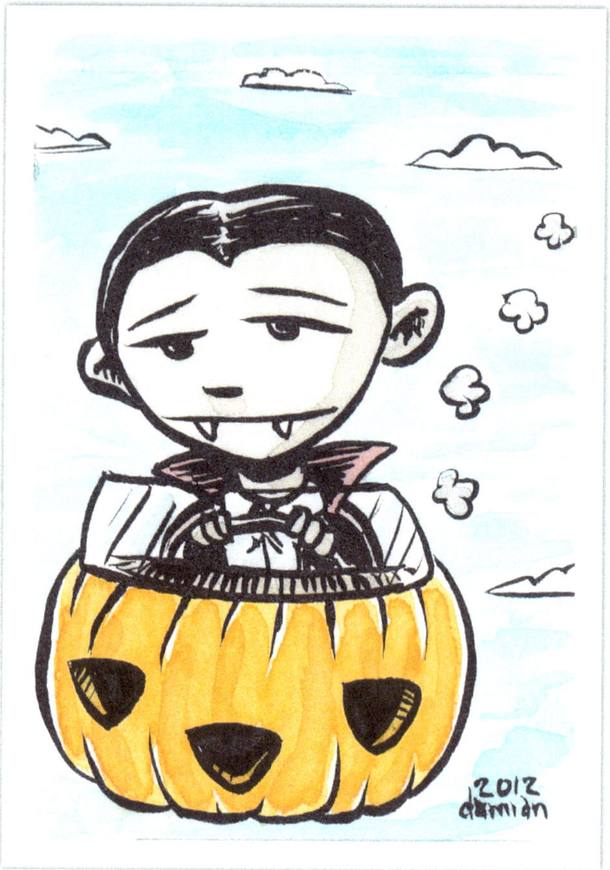
2012
damian

“dracula driving a flying pumpkin”

(ink & watercolour)

i think i just broke halloween.

(bamboopaper on ipad)

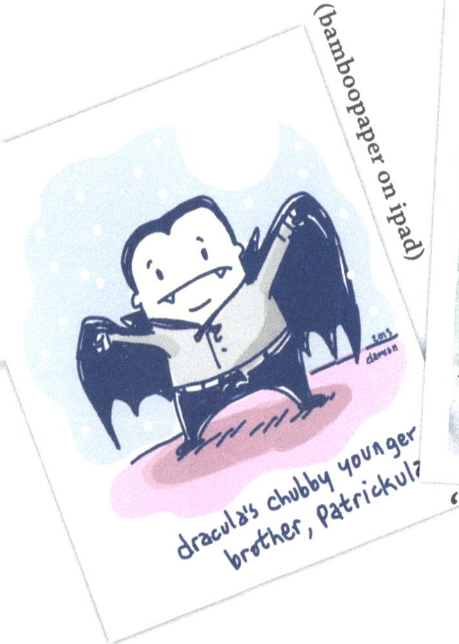
2013
damian
dracula's chubby younger brother, patrickula

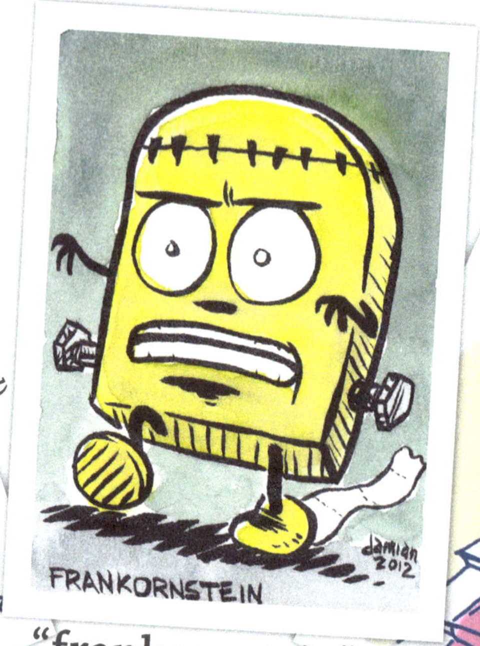
damian
2012
FRANKORNSTEIN

“frankornstein”

(ink & watercolour)

(bamboopaper on ipad)

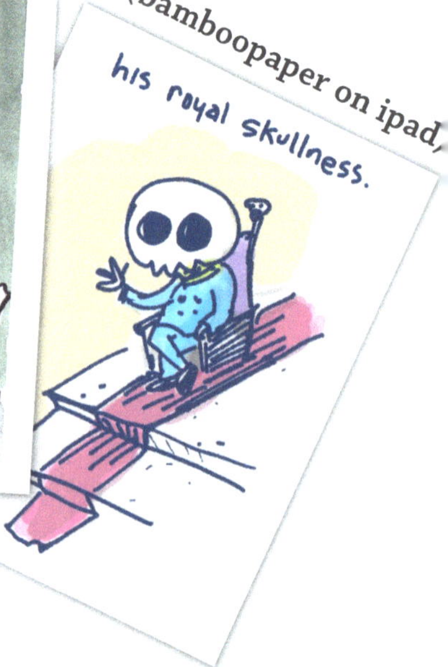
his royal skullness.

"yes, master"
(finger painted in adobe ideas
on ipad...in bed, in the middle
of the night... when i had
trouble sleeping...
"good thinking, damian...
draw something creepy to help
yourself sleep")

" the loneliest hat rack"

"the loneliest hat rack"
(adobe ideas on ipad)

"welcome to the fewture"
(ink & watercolour w/b&w ink/pre-watercolour image shown in back)

"flagrant-disregard-for-the-law-of-gravity-bot"
(bamboopaper on ipad)

"nomadbot"
(ink & watercolour)

the food groups & hiragana?

i have made a much more concerted effort to learn to read and write japanese this past year. as such, i had begun to draw my lunch to practice japanese hiragana characters, spelling out words that i knew and turning my meals into live characters apparently at the same time....

とりにく (TORI NIKU) すし (SUSHI) LITERALLY... BIRD MEAT

bok! bok!

myLunch July 16 2012 damian

"bok bok" (ink & watercolour)

みそらめん (MISO RAMEN)   りんご (RINGO [APPLE])

EVERYBODY LOVES RAMEN

damian 2012

"my lunch - based on the tv show" (ink & watercolour)

なべ "NABE"

とりにく TORI NIKU   BOK! BOK!   もち MOCHI   BOK! BOK!

しいたけ SHIITAKE   えのき ENOKI

July 24th 2012   "SUPPER - NABE" damian

"nabe" (ink & watercolour)

let's meet some of the other food groups encountered along the way shall we?

42

VEGGIE DOG

"veggie dog" (ink & watercolour)

protein...

sadly, pretty soon things just sort of devolved from Hiragana practice into drawing my lunch...er.. sort of... I mean, if it were to come to life...and learn the deadly art of the way of the ninja, like our friend below....

"silent eggssassin"
(ink & watercolour)

"pancakes"
(ink & watercolour)

"toast of the town"
(ink & watercolour)

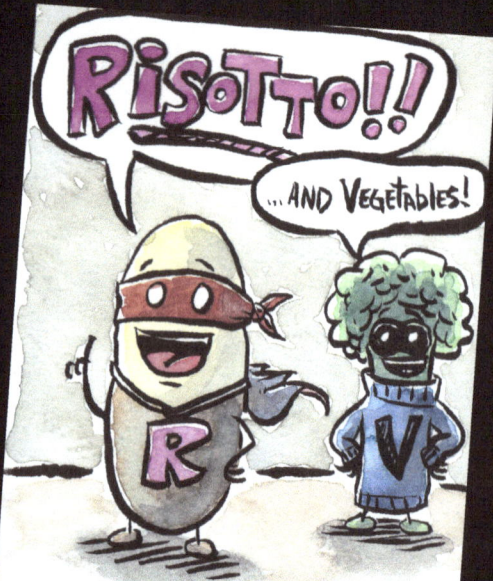

"risotto & vegetables"
(ink & watercolour)

"wild rice"
(ink & watercolour)

"superfoods explained"
(ink & watercolour)

"veggie crossing"
(ink & watercolour)

"sour advice"
(ink & watercolour)

...and of course, the fifth food group: marshmallow.

"monsieur mallow suddenly realized he
didn't belong with koko."
(ink & watercolour)
marshmallows with self doubt?
sadly, not even a hot chocolate can make
you feel better after that...

an ode to tea

tea, tea, oh how can you be
such a wonderful thing that's been given to me
your dried leaves in water, unravel, expand
unleashing tea-ish flavour upon my demand,
filled with caffeine, and a loving intention,
in grade 7 a stink bomb got me a detention,
grown in a tree , covered with aphids and dirt
pre rinsing your leaves can definitely not hurt,
Gong Fu tea in China, in Japan they add rice,
in the warehouse the leaves might be pooped on by mice,
yet i savour the flavour, the aroma, the blend,
write stupid rhymes, and then to you send,
my message today of tea, here's the crux
please don't believe those who say that it sucks,
for they're wolves in sheep's clothing and will steal 5 bucks;
in return give you coffee 'cuz they own starbucks.
-damian willcox

"in hot water"
(sketchbook pro on ipad)

MISTER TEA

"mister tea"
(ink & watercolour)

japan

this is a photo i took of a lonely street in japan at approximately 4:30 a.m. on january 1, 2013. after visiting another city we discovered that the trains there were no longer running, though we very luckily made it home on the very last train of the night from another location after a fast paced and chaotic taxi ride to the next city. happy new year.

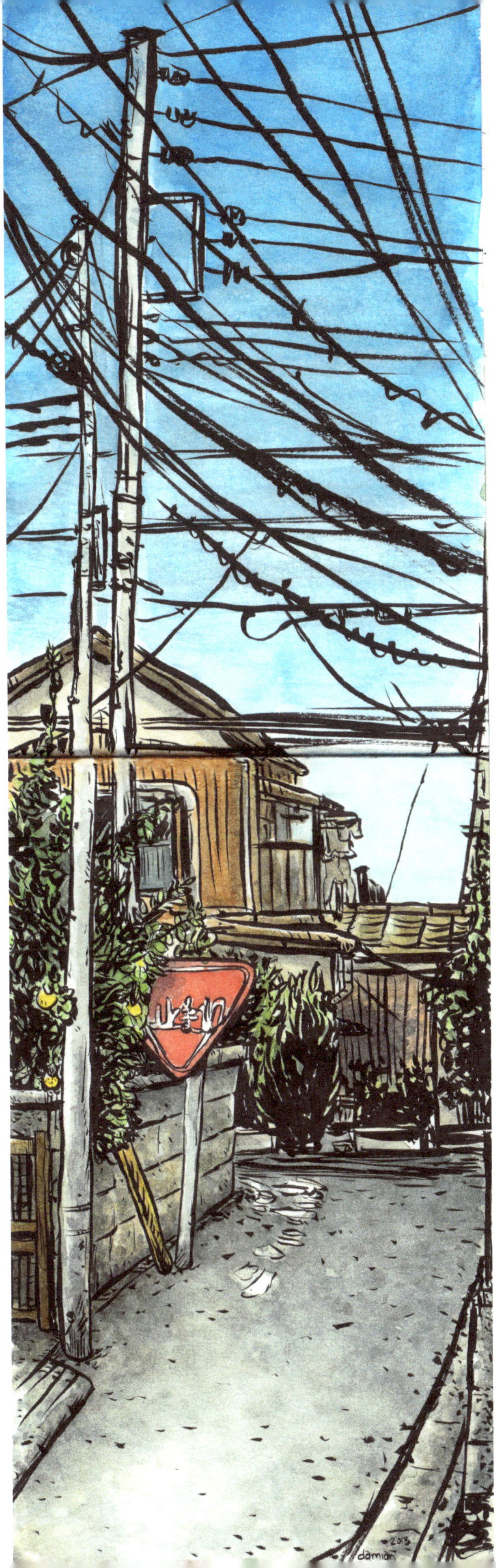

"end of the road"

(ink & watercolour)

this is a drawing of the end of the street from my mother in law's doorstep. i have seen this particular street a large number of times over the years, and just love the character it has. although it took several years, i did finally make good on my vow to make a drawing of it.

the photo below is of me riding a rubber chain driven bicycle (see the comic in my other book *dorkboy: questionable characters*) with mostly flat tires, and a basket on the front that has been around since my wife's junior high school days. she is seen comfortably scooting ahead of me... on a side note, i am 6'-1", which is in fact much taller than your average junior high school girl in japan...and their bicycle.

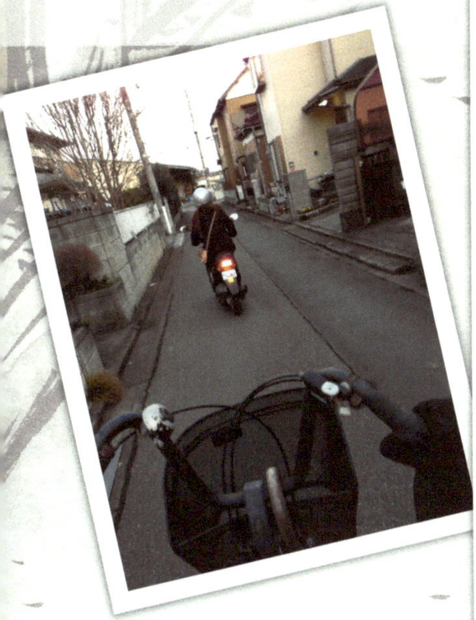

akasaka shrine

i was lucky to be able to meet up with a group of fellow sketching friends in tokyo thanks to the connectivity of the internet, and the common bond of drawing. i have overlaid my sketches on to the photos of the location i was attempting to draw to try and give them some context. we met in akasaka, not to be confused with the place i almost went to: asakusa. shown here: the shrine in akasaka.

"vending"

a sketch of two of the many vending machines that can be seen everywhere in japan...

"salaryman's lunch"

akasaka has a number of offices, and so the "salarymen" were pouring into the streets in search of lunch while i sketched this...

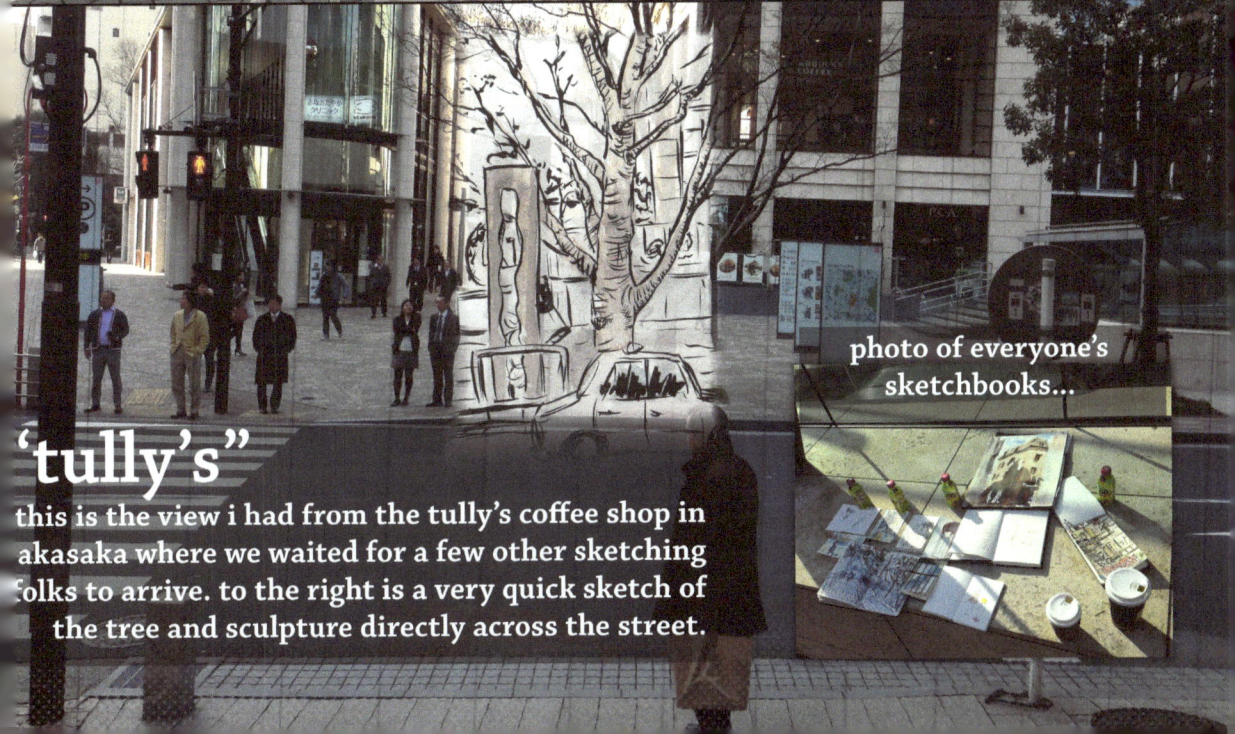

'tully's'

this is the view i had from the tully's coffee shop in akasaka where we waited for a few other sketching folks to arrive. to the right is a very quick sketch of the tree and sculpture directly across the street.

photo of everyone's sketchbooks...

"Soaking my feet in a road side foot bath on the volcanic island of Sakurajima"

HAPPY YEAR OF THE SN̶¢AKE!

2013

"year of the cake?"
(ink & watercolour on small paper)
once again, the new year involved plenty of
exploring japan, as evidenced in my photos here.

"Takachiho gorge" 2012·12·27

“the life of spy…”

(ink & watercolour)

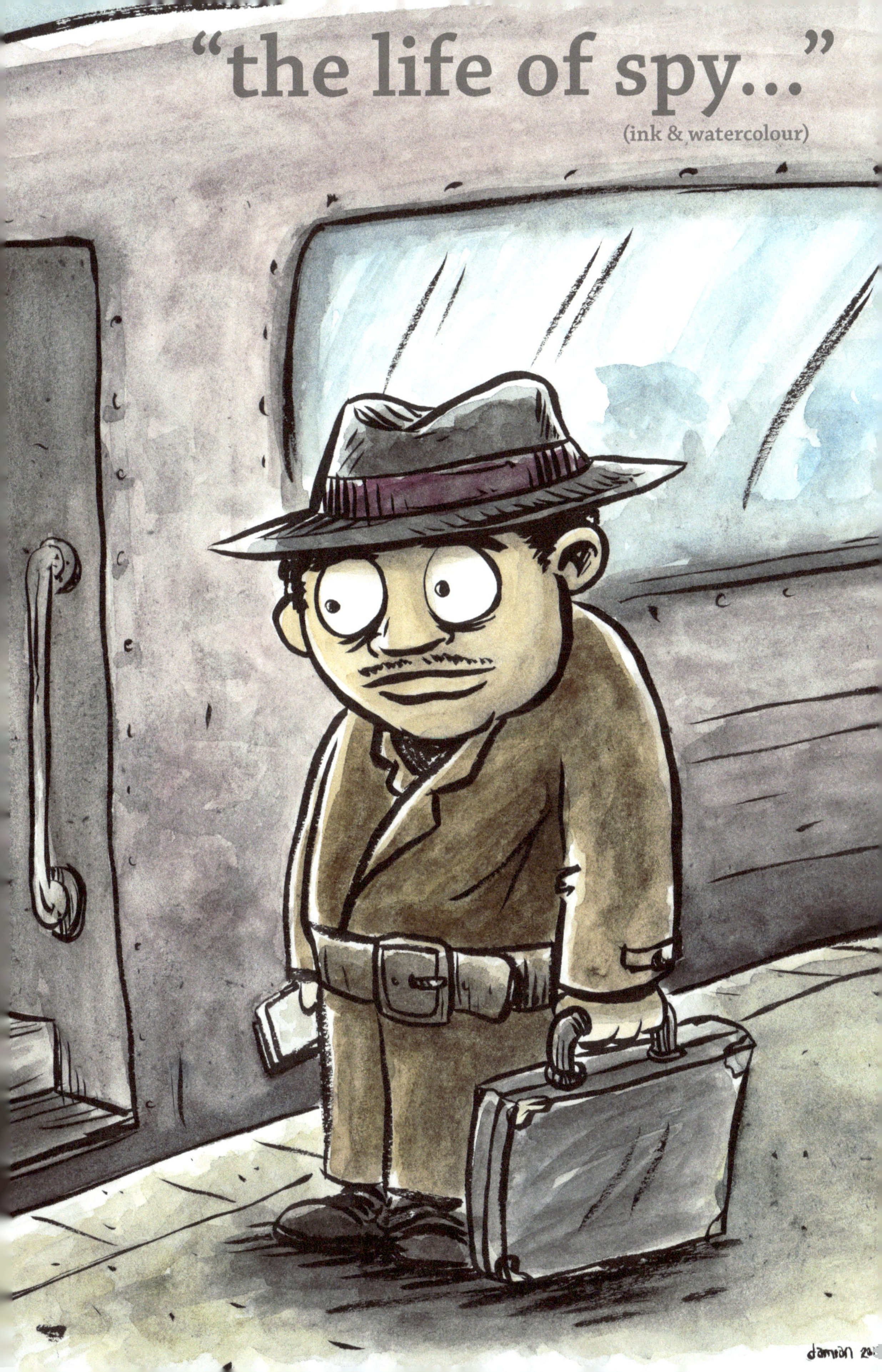
damian

"...and the ladies of espionage."

"no, mr. bond...i don't believe we have met"
(adobe ideas on ipad)
i was raised on 007 movies growing up, but comedy spoofs like
"get smart" became an even stronger staple of my childhood where
the beauty was the brains of the operation, much like these next
illustrations.

"they said to never look back"
(adobe illustrator)

"the inconspicuous spy"
(adobe ideas on ipad)

"spring"
(adobe ideas on ipad)

"make like a tree"
(adobe ideas on ipad)

"step two: taking names"
(adobe ideas on ipad)

"winds of change"
(autodesk sketchbook ink on ipad)

and of course, heroes of another type...

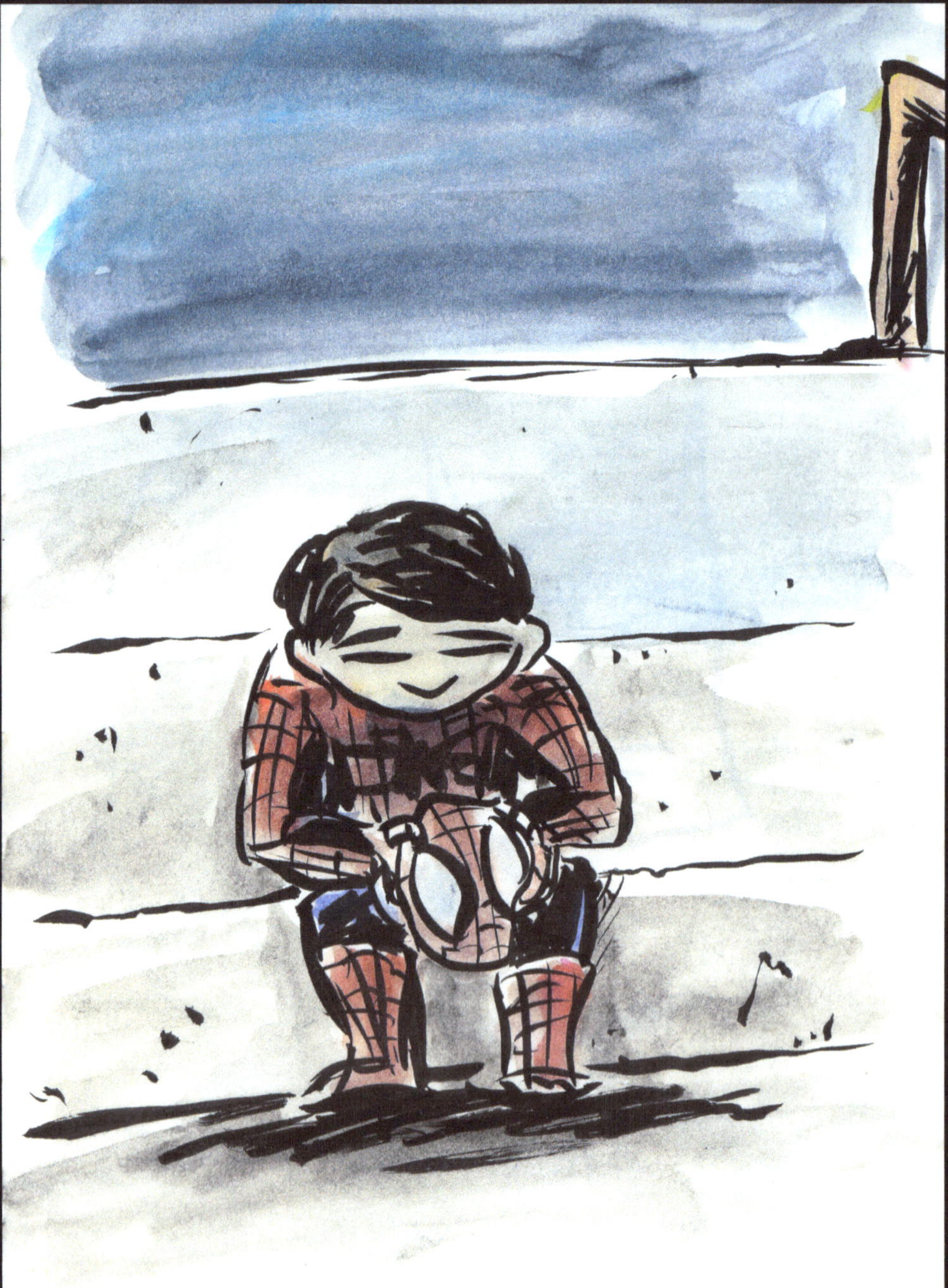

“first day on the new job”

"everyone wants to wear the cape...but no
one wants to save the world"

(ink & watercolour)

Wild animals...

"arrrggtopus"
(ink & watercolour)

FREE COMIC BOOK DAY COMICS
- EPISODE FIVE -

the thought of people tattooing my artwork onto themselves scares me - mostly because i picture myself needing to apologize for it for the rest of their life.

that said, the super amazing arthur chocholacek (see comic from him visiting me on free comic book day to the left) went ahead and did just this and permanently infused my "arrgtopus" (top left) into his arm! (above)

arm courtesy of arthur chocholacek

arthur courtesy of arthur's mom.

tattoo courtesy of dan morgan, pirates alley studio in olds, ab, canada

...and "real" animals.

i seem to turn every inanimate object i draw into a living
thing, so it's probably good that i make time for drawing
some "actual" living animals once in a while also.

"the bark is actually better than the bite"
(ink & watercolour)
um...i may have even drawn this one on canada day.
(eh)

"now, flap!"
(ink & watercolour)
you will notice a different texture on this particular one. this is due to the
fact that i accidentally painted it on the back of the cover to my watercolour
sketchbook....i noticed this right about the time i was almost finished.

"soo-weet!"
(bamboopaper on ipad)

"le cochon et une petite
bicyclette"
(ink & watercolour)

"today is that day"
(ink & watercolour)

So, uh... whatcha doing, master?

You look like you're having fun! are you having fun? are you? are you being a good boy?

HOLY CRAP, LYCHEE!! YOU'RE TALKING!!

that's right, master! you're so smart!! good boy!

this is so amazing! ...but...but why are you talking like that?

Like what, master? I'm talking like you, yes you!!

What? I don't talk like that!

You don't?

NO!

oh... well, maybe this will ring a bell...

WHO's a good girl? you are! you are, muffin! that's right... wanna go for a widdle walk? do ya? do ya? good girl, muffin!!

OK!! Enough already!!

BARK! BARK! BARK!

HEY!! WHAT THE? Let's speak english, you know I don't speak dog!!

so, hey... umm... I was thinking maybe we can find you a hobby... or... but... she was really just... uh...

Woof! woof! oh good, the smart one's back!

END

..and some comics for or because of our dog "lychee".

THE TWO SPEEDS OF

MY DOG LYCHEE!

SPEED ONE...

ZZZ

ZERO (ASLEEP)
90% OF THE TIME

SPEED TWO...

BARK BARK BARK BARK BARK BARK BARK BARK BARK BARK BARK BARK BARK BARK BARK BARK BARK BARK BARK BARK BARK BARK BARK BARK BARK BARK BARK BARK BARK BARK BARK BARK BARK BARK BARK BARK BARK

500%
(DOG HURRICANE)
10% OF THE TIME

master while you were making fun of me in your comic I made you a present...

damian 2013

facebark

REX: Woof Woof Woof Woof Woof Woof Woof Woof

FIDO shared a picture...

Misty changed her relationship status to "It's complicated"

COOPER NEEDS 100 Coins To get out of catville

SPOT liked a photo

Rover was tagged in a family photo

damian

Places to pee

places to drink

"a drawing of Canada by my dog"

"bokarista"
(bamboopaper on ipad)

"Mostly Harmless #2"
(adobe illustrator)
i drew this cover image for another "damian"
that was putting together his own 'zines
several years back. to this day, it is still my
favourite teddy bear drawing.

"can i get some ice for my
drink, please?"
(ink & watercolour)

68

about the artist...

damian willcox is an award nominated cartoonist that has been publishing his comics and art in print and online for over fifteen years.

During that time he has also written the Too Much Coffee Man Opera with Shannon Wheeler, survived his comics getting TV series related interest from Hollywood types, and has even appeared in a National Chinese television show as a 'wealthy foreigner'.

He currently lives in Calgary, Alberta, Canada and spends his days with his wonderful wife Miyuki and nutty dog Lychee.

end note.

I've been making comics for quite a few years now, and am to this day still shocked and surprised by the support I get from fans like you.

I want to say thank you so much for picking up this book, and for being a hugely motivating factor in my work, I really appreciate it and it means a lot.

thanks,

♥damian

"I love you, man!" 2012-12-29, 3:33 pm. Sanmesse, Nichinan, Japan

www.dorkboycomics.com
damian@dorkboycomics.com

find me...

twitter: @dorkboycomics
google+:   plus.dorkboycomics.com
facebook: facebook.com/damiandraws
tumblr: dorkboycomics.tumblr.com

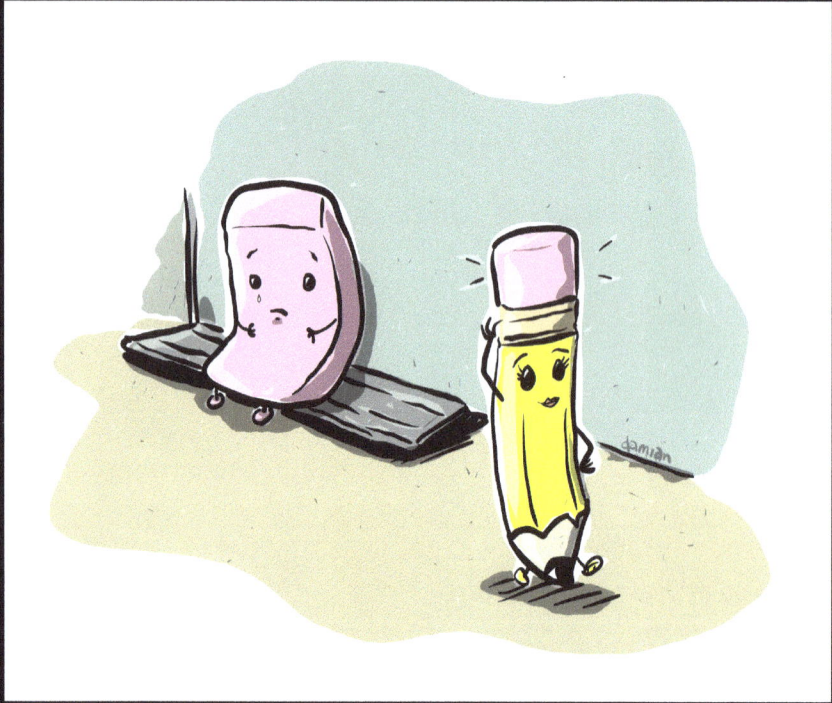

"i can't erase you from my mind"
(adobe illustrator)

see you again soon,
and thank you.

♥damian

whew!
I'm
pooped...

www.ingramcontent.com/pod-product-compliance
Lightning Source LLC
Chambersburg PA
CBHW061356090426
42739CB00003B/40